A Beginner's Guide to the Early Realm of Colonial Print Culture in India.

Making sense of the curious nature of early print in Bengal (1780-1820).

TAPATI BHARADWAJ

Copyright © 2015 Tapati Bharadwaj

All rights reserved.

ISBN: 9384281042
ISBN-13: 978-9384281045

DEDICATION

Calcutta, the 12th Jan. 1788.   By Order
                                                             G. H. BARLO[W]

For SALE at the CIRCULATING LIBRARY.

Some very elegant Bound

QUARTO and OCTAVO BIBLES and PRAYER B[OOKS]
of different sizes.

Also, some complete Sets of

EUROPE BOUND MERCHANTS BOOK[S]
And a variety of STATIONARY, in good order.

CONTENTS

	Acknowledgments	i
1	INTRODUCTION: HOW DID NATIVES READ?	3
2	IMPERIAL PRINT	9
3	GRAMMAR BOOKS	15
4	NATHANIEL HALHED'S *A GRAMMAR OF THE BENGAL LANGUAGE*	22
5	THE FIRST REALM OF PRINT	35
6	EAST INDIA COMPANY SPONSORED PRINT AND ORIENTALISM	40
7	SCRIBAL CULTURE	48
8	DIRT AND SQUALOR AND PRINT	58
9	A WESTERNISED WHITE CITY IN CALCUTTA	62
10	BOOK ADVERTISEMENTS AND PRINT	65
11	MULTILINGUAL TEXTS	71
12	CAN UTILITARIANISM MAKE THE NATIVES HAPPY?	81
13	HOW NATIVE FONT WERE MADE	88
14	NATIVE MASTERY	97

By Order
C. H. BARLO[W]

Calcutta, the 12th Jan. 1788.

[Persian/Urdu text]

[Bengali/Assamese tabular content with numerical entries]

For SALE at the CIRCULATING LIBRARY.

Some very elegant Bound
QUARTO and OCTAVO BIBLES and PRAYER B[OOKS]
of different sizes.

Also, some complete Sets of
EUROPE BOUND MERCHANTS BOOK[S]
And a variety of STATIONARY, in good order.

ACKNOWLEDGMENTS

This book, on early colonial print in Calcutta, India, would not have bene possible without the kind support that I received at two libraries. I wish to thank everyone at the National Library, Kolkata for making my archival research possible. I also want to thank everyone in the library facilities at Loyola University, Chicago for making it possible to have access to a lot of research resources.
Even as we celebrate the advent of the non-textual book, there is also need to remember the materiality of the printed text.

Calcutta, the 12th Jan. 1788.

By Order
C. H. BARLO[W]

For SALE at the CIRCULATING LIBRARY.

Some very elegant Bound
QUARTO and OCTAVO BIBLES and PRAYER BO[OKS]
of different sizes.

Also, some complete Sets of
EUROPE BOUND MERCHANTS BOOK[S]
And a variety of STATIONARY, in good order.

1 INTRODUCTION: HOW DID NATIVES READ?

At the turn of the century, books made their way into Indian society and began to displace a manuscript culture. Natives started to read, make use of and negotiate their lives through printed texts. Moreover, the press initiated a shift in the very nature of how texts were to be written, preserved and disseminated. In fact, it initiated a shift in the very method of writing, a shift that involved cultural habits – Indians would sit on the floor and write, unlike Europeans who used tables and chairs. Nathaniel Halhed describes it in the following manner: "As they have neither chairs nor tables, their posture in writing is very different from ours: they sit upon their heels, or sometimes upon their hams, while their left hand held open serves as a desk whereon to lay the paper on which they write, which is kept in its place by the thumb: so that they never write on a large sheet of paper without folding it down to a very small surface."[1] It is fascinating to conjecture as to how exactly the change to print took place. As more and more natives had access to printed texts, that which had been the privilege of a particular class of people, now became democratized. Now, a large canvas of Indian society had access to printed books. How did it feel to be able to touch printed paper and read, and be aware that many others across the land were also reading the same text? Indians closely interacted with the Britishers and learnt their social manners, learning how the technology worked. They also learnt the different uses that print could come into.

    A basic fundamental question that keeps on arising over and over again is on how the realm of print in colonial Bengal (between 1780 and

---

[1] Nathaniel Halhed, *A Grammar of the Bengal Language*, 1778. Reprint, ed. R. C. Alston (England: The Scolar Press, 1969), p. 2.

1800) perpetuated and embodied power? Was it such a simple process of shifting ship loads of people and technology across the oceans and settling them down in Calcutta? What was it that motivated people to move themselves from England, apart from the obvious monetary attraction? Examining a few moments (and a few people involved) in the process of technological exchange will allow us a more nuanced understanding of what is usually written off as mere mimicry by most postcolonial theorists.

George Gordon was one of the printers who came and started a printing press in Calcutta; he was also the only printer who was professionally trained as a printer before his departure from England.[2] Gordon was the nephew of one of the most eminent eighteenth century London printers, William Strahan, who was also the king's printer, and a friend of Samuel Johnson and Benjamin Franklin. He

---

[2] For more see Graham Shaw, *Printing in Calcutta before 1800* (Oxford: Oxford University Press, 1981), pp. 48-50.

was recommended by his uncle to the Court of Directors of the East India Company and was the only licensed printer by the Company. Another well known printer was Charles Wilkins who joined the East India Company in 1770 as a writer; he was well versed in Persian and Bengali and made the earliest known types in Bengali.[3] He was also invited to establish a printing press for the Company so that it could print its own official documents. He was appointed as the first superintendent of the Honourable Company's Press in December 1778. The press was in Malda where the Company's factories were located, and Wilkins was also the supervisor of these factories. Here Wilkins made a set of Persian types. The Company's press was removed to Calcutta in 1781 where Wilkins was transferred as the Persian and Bengali translator to the Committee of Revenue. The first work to be printed here was his own *A Translation of a royal grant of land by one of the ancient Rajaas of Hindostan*; Francis Gladwin's translation of *Ayeen Akbari* was the last work to be printed

---

[3] For more see Shaw, pp. 69-71.

under his supervision in 1783. After Wilkins left for Benaras in December 1783, Gladwin succeeded him as the superintendent of the press in January of 1784. All of these people were involved in the process of empire making, meticulously learning the languages and the habits of the natives. Some of them carried with them the best of British civilization and imparted it to the natives.

It would therefore be a more meaningful discussion if we understood power as operating in a more sophisticated manner rather than simply being imposed upon others in a binary fashion. Those Britishers who traveled to India were people who were part and parcel of the Juggernaut of empire making and they were blood and flesh people and not necessarily heinously mean or cruel. The intellectual brahminical elite allowed themselves to be participants in this process, only because they were involved in a new epistemic shift; the tradeoff must have been fair. It is rather simplistic to construe the natives as being overpowered or incapable of resistance of any sort. The sheer fascination with the new-ness of the social and technological aspects of print culture might have been, after all, irresistible.

For SALE *at the* CIRCULATING LIBRARY.

Some very elegant Bound
QUARTO and OCTAVO BIBLES and PRAYER B[...]
of different sizes.

Alſo, ſome complete Sets of
EUROPE BOUND MERCHANTS BOOK[...]
And a variety of STATIONARY, in good order.

2 IMPERIAL PRINT

In the last two decades of the eighteenth century, a realm of print culture evolved in Calcutta serving the needs of empire. The East India Company used this realm——which printed news, gossip, Oriental scholarship, literary journals——to establish and maintain its control over the territories. Moreover, the printed scholarship of the scholar-administrators of the East India Company reveals their belief that print technology was a step into modernity, a move away from Indian scribal culture. Print culture, in Bengal pre-1800 was produced for a non-native audience, that was also located in Europe. As content determines how interpretations take place, I have argued that the white settlers read in order to create a sense of imperial identity and thus, print technology in the colonial context was never innocent. The realm of readership was local and also global. The small group of non-native residents in Bengal was connected with Europe and each other through print. The capacity to imagine themselves as part of empire and to define their identity as imperial subjects was made possible through the to-and-fro movement of texts.

Such a notion of a realm that is invested with power and made possible by print borrows from concepts of cartography. Maps portray a sense of space that is never value-free. Maps do not depict reality with scientific accuracy and objectivity. Brian Harley writes that "cartography is primarily a form of political discourse concerned with the acquisition and maintenance of power."[4] According to Harley:

> Compilation, generalization, classification, formation into hierarchies, and standardization of geographical data, far from being mere "neutral" technical activities, involve power-knowledge relations at work. Just as the disciplinary institutions described by Foucault—prisons, schools,

---

[4] Brian Harley, *The New Nature of Maps; Essays in the History of Cartography* (Baltimore: John Hopkins University Press, 2002), p. 57.

armies, factories—serve to normalize human beings, so too the workshop of the map-maker can be seen as normalizing the phenomena of place and territory in creating a sketch of a made world that society desired.⁵

Maps are "preeminently a language of power, not of protest"⁶ and this is most aptly evident in those maps that portray imperial conquest as British cartographers drew maps that reiterated British power. Ian Barrow makes a similar argument when he writes that during the British colonial period, maps were the most effective resources the British had in order to legitimize their roles as a colonial power.⁷ The territories they colonized were portrayed as inevitably British, and intrinsic to the British empire. For example, John Tallis' *Illustrated Atlas and Modern History of the World* included maps of British India that were

---

⁵ Ibid., p. 22.

⁶ Ibid., p. 5.

⁷ Ian Barrow, *Making History, Drawing Territory. British Mapping in India, c. 1756-1905* (New Delhi, Oxford University Press, 2003).

accompanied by a text that explained how British power was established over the colony.[8] Maps mimetically represented geographical territory alongside a rendition of a history of how the space was colonized. The power of maps lies in the fact that they can recreate territory in a particular manner through elisions; for example, a map of Calcutta in the 1800s depicted all Indians as peasants or servants and established the land as meant for the English. Maps, thus, portrayed the existing ideologies that were inflected with a sense of imperial legitimacy. And like maps, the realm of printed texts that emerged in the first phase of colonial print, that is pre-1800, reiterated a similar notion of colonial superiority whereby the introduction of print technology was construed as an inevitable move towards modernity and progress.

    The non native population of rulers could live by identifying themselves as separate from the natives; by the end of the eighteenth century, realms of institutional power were

---

[8] John Tallis, *Illustrated Atlas and Modern History of the World* (New York: J. &F. Tallis, 1851).

established in the colonies and in the process, imperial identity was formed intrinsic to maintaining a territory. Print culture was one such import that made colonial control possible. The realm of print was both spatial (through acts of reading) and a geo-physical domain (the realm of printers and type foundries). This was akin to many other realms that emerged in the last two decades of the eighteenth century — the development of Calcutta as a westernized city, cartography and the use of maps by the East India Company, and lastly, western habits of consumption in the colonies. The print induced communication circuit was one such realm which existed in conjunction with the other institutional and disciplinary realms.

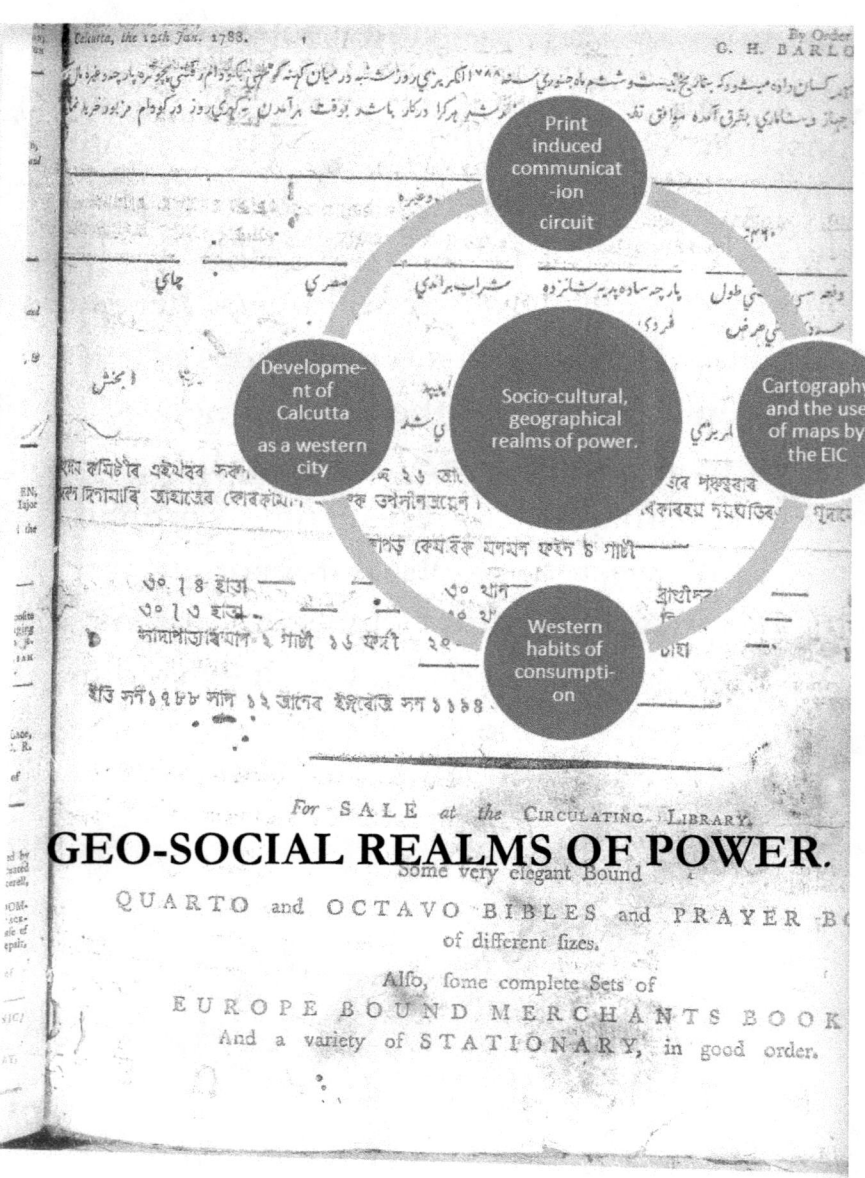

GEO-SOCIAL REALMS OF POWER.

3 GRAMMAR BOOKS

The use of print in the colonies was not inevitable as manuscripts were used as well as handwritten notices and circulars. Initially print was seen as a threat and many printers who attempted to print were deported to Europe. The works of Orientalist scholars are well known, but what need was there for grammar books and dictionaries to be printed and publicized and what part did the dissemination of printed material play in the debate of empire building in Bengal? Government patronage did determine the nature of print in the early years and for the publication of works on philology and grammar.[9] Patterns of dissemination and

---

[9] Miles Ogborn, *India Ink, Script and Print in the making of the English East India Company* (Chicago: University of Chicago Press, 1997), p. 2120.

distribution were also determined by government finance.[10] Printed texts were circulated, enabling an imperial sphere of 'social communication' to be constructed that included readers and writers in India and in England, but this cannot necessarily be assumed to be a "consensual interpretative community"[11] for natives were not equal collaborators in this enterprise. These grammar books, legal texts and translations of religious texts were printed, placing them within an "imperial circuit" of production, dissemination and reception.[12] Moreover, the needs of empire building determined why grammar books were printed, and did not necessarily reflect the needs of the natives. Subsequently, these grammar books – meant to aid in standardizing Indian languages -- did become the definitive norm in India.

When examining the nature of how grammar books emerged in Calcutta, written

---

[10] Ibid., p. 221.

[11] Ibid., p. 223.

[12] Ibid., p. 225.

on the same lines as grammar books in England, and the complicated logic behind them, it would be relevant to understand how grammar books evolved in England in a completely different context — or for that matter, how the emergence of the printing press helped in standardizing the English language. When William Caxton set up his printing press around 1476, it was about fifty years since the Chancery English had been adopted as the standard, based on the London and the East Midland dialect. Caxton's press aided in making this dialect of English as the norm. Caxton set up his printing press in Westminster close to Parliament, and decided to print in the vernacular, realizing the economic prospects of the new venture. This was a smart move, as there had been other printers who had set up presses on Oxford and St. Albans, and had failed. These printers had published academic books in Latin, not realizing that such books could easily be available through trade with the Continent.[13]

---

[13] Norman Blake, *Caxton and his World* (London: Andre Deutsch, 1969).

It was largely for economic reasons that Caxton was searching for a "relatively stable language variety that could serve a superregional function to speakers of different dialects."[14] He used a dialect that was the most widely accepted written variety, and used by the literate segments of society, which constituted his own intended audience. By the end of the fifteenth century, "economic motivations contributed significantly to earlier linguistic and political ones in the standardization of the language."[15] Writing dictionaries and grammar books were some of the processes that were involved in standardizing a language. The first dictionaries were written in the early eighteenth century and were meant to include new, unfamiliar words that had entered the English language over the centuries; dictionaries were needed to explain these words to the common user or to the well-educated[16] and did not include those words that were in everyday use.

---

[14] Terttu Nevalainen and Ingrid Tieken-Boon van Ostade. "Standardisation," in *A History of the English Language*. eds. Richard Hogg and David Denison (Cambridge: Cambridge University Press, 1992), pp. 271-311; p. 278.

[15] Ibid., p. 278.

[16] Ibid., p. 283.

Nathan Bailey's *Dictionarium Britannicum*, that was written in 1730, was the first dictionary to include all words and was subsequently used as a source for Johnson's *Dictionary of the English Language* (1755).[17] Early grammarians resorted to Latin grammar to provide them with a model and English grammar was not considered as an object worthy of study for its own sake till 1653 with the publication of Wallis's *Grammatica Linguae Anglicanae*. English grammar was treated like Latin, and emphasis was given to its morphology. Grammarians of the eighteenth century wanted to fix the language, only to realize that a living language could not be fixed. Lindley Murray's grammar book (first published in 1795) came to be looked upon as a handbook of English grammar. English grammar books were taken as a model for grammar books on native languages and the need to write such books were driven by the needs of empire and the East India Company.

The nature of how these grammar books

---

[17] Ibid., p. 284.

in the colonial context came to be written is symptomatic of Tony Ballantyne's argument that imperial knowledge was often disembodied from the socio-traditional context from within which they emerged. Ballantyne argues that colonial states gathered knowledge from a wide range of sources about the colonies and printing was crucial to the systematization and dissemination of colonial knowledge.[18] This form of codified knowledge was the basis of the day to day operation of colonial power, but "the processes by which they were created profoundly altered the knowledge they recorded, disembodying these traditions, wrenching them free of the traditional social contexts of knowledge transmissions to revalue them as an aid to the operation of imperial authority."[19] Recent histories of empire look at the connections between the role of colonial knowledge and the establishment of colonial authority.[20]

---

[18] Tony Ballantyne, "What Difference does Colonialism Make? Reassessing Print and Social Change in an age of global imperialism," in *Agent of Change: Print Culture Studies After Elizabeth L. Eisenstein*, eds. Sabrina Baron, Eric Lindquist and Eleanor Shevlin (Amherst: University of Massachusetts Press, 2007).

[19] Ibid., p. 345.

[20] As printing was "central" to the working of the modern colonial state, it has

Even as colonial authorities used print to exercise power, what is not very clear is the nature of power? It is easy to write off colonial power as being absolute but power in this instance – as the preceding analysis has shown – was far from being totalitarian. Colonial authority did not operate in a binary of absolute coercion and pliant submission and the natives – for that matter, the intellectual elites in many instances – participated in the dissemination of colonial authority. Those who were being ruled allowed themselves to be a part of this process of technological exchange, even as it was used to make them subordinates.

"become an important point of debate in the scholarship on modern empire building"; print was an important tool for "colonial administrators, missionaries and social reformers" and was reconceptualized in the colonial situation. Ibid., p. 343.

4 NATHANIEL HALHED'S *A GRAMMAR OF THE BENGAL LANGUAGE*

Grammar books on Indian languages were meant to aid the East India Company. In order to maintain order in the colonies, it was essential to learn the languages of the Indians; this territorial domain of the colonies could be controlled by mastering the realm of native languages and codifying them in grammar books. Grammar books like Francis Gladwin's *The Persian Moonshe* (1795), *A Vocabulary, Persian, Arabic, and English* (1797), which aided the British to learn Persian and Bengali, were printed by English printing presses to cater to the needs of the administrators of the Company. This realm of texts was specific to the English community in Calcutta, and was meant to aid in trade and rule. Such texts play a similar role as that of colonial cartography in the processes of British empire building. As Ian Barrow argues, the mapping of India and the creation of colonial territory helped to build British national identity.[21] Colonial cartography depicted histories of British territorial possession and these histories helped the British to remake themselves as legitimate rulers while also reinforcing the notion of a British national identity. Grammar books, for the most, made colonial possession more legitimate. One of the first books to be written was Nathaniel Halhed's *A Grammar of the Bengal Language*, in 1778. In 1783, a reviewer in *The English Review* wrote that the "settlements in the East" deserve the "chief attention" of Britain. A printed grammar book would draw public attention to the language spoken by "millions of industrious British subjects" and would also aid in the "proper management of the commercial, military and revenue departments in Bengal."[22]

---

[21] Ian Barrow, *Making History, Drawing Territory: British Mapping in India, c. 1756-1905* (New Delhi: Oxford University Press, 2003).

[22] "Review of Halhed's *A Grammar of the Bengal Language*", *The English Review*, p. 5-14.

Printing a grammar book would allow for better communication between the government and the natives, enabling benevolent rule. Print was an extension of the state and the state defined itself through print. For Halhed:

> The wisdom of the British Parliament has within these few years taken a decisive part in the internal policy and civil administration of its Asiatic territories…. Much however still remains for the completion of this grand work; and we may reasonably presume, that one of its most important desiderata is the cultivation of a right understanding and of a general medium of intercourse between Government, and its subjects; between the natives of Europe who are to rule, and the Inhabitants of India who are to obey.[23]

---

[23] Halhed, *A Grammar*, pp. i-ii

If the British were to rule, then print would play an important function in making that rule possible. Halhed draws a comparison between the present British conquest of Bengal and the colonial desire to learn the language of the natives with a historical antecedent, when the Romans, " a people of little learning and less taste, [who] had no sooner conquered Greece than they applied themselves to the study of Greek."[24] Learning the language of Bengal would allow the rulers to explain the benevolent principles of that Legislation whose decrees they enforce[d]"; the desire was to "convince" and persuade the natives" while they commanded.[25] The economic imperatives were enormous and would be no less beneficial to the Revenue Department.[26] In all respects, the printed grammar book was a means of inevitable social progress in the colonies.

By the latter part of the eighteenth century, print culture was seen as being

---

[24] Ibid., p. 1.

[25] Ibid., pp. i-ii.

[26] Ibid., p. xv.

superior to other forms of communication. The move was towards codifying into print all the existing knowledge systems documented in a scribal-manuscript culture and this was construed as a shift into inevitable progress. Halhed draws attention to the mechanical aspects of print technology. The book, he writes, was to be seen as "extraordinary" and an "instance of mechanic abilities" and meant for the British public whose "curiosity" would be "strongly excited by the beautiful characters" that were displayed in the text.[27] Making Bengali fonts was not easy as the Bengali letters were "very difficult to be imitated in steel." Halhed erroneously credits Mr. Wilkins, an employee of the East India Company as being successful by undertaking the various occupations of "Metallurgist, the Engraver, the Founder and the Printer,"[28] and completely misrepresents the fact that natives were also involved; in fact, Panchanan Karmakar played an important role along with Wilkins. The process that was involved, of

---

[27] Halhed, *A Grammar*, p. xxiii.

[28] Ibid., p. xxiv.

creating types in steel, of transferring and establishing clarity to the illegible, handwritten manuscripts—where the "inaccuracy of their writings" frequently deviated from their original forms—imparted a sense of authenticity and fixity to the act of writing.[29] Technology is celebrated as it has the capacity to represent even the most difficult of languages. Print technology made pure the existing state of social affairs; the various "impositions and forgeries with which Bengal at present abounds," Halhed wrote, would be done away with.[30]

Halhed has to be seen as working within the existing ideological notions of empire-making. Britain defined itself as civilized and modern by characterizing India and its languages as primitive. British rule was conceived as benevolent, a system of government, made possible and facilitated through print unlike scribal culture. The British nation was interested in "marking the progress of her

---

[29] Ibid., p .3.

[30] Ibid., p. xxiv.

conquests by a liberal communication of Arts and Sciences, rather than by the effusion of blood."[31] The "poorer classes of people" were oppressed in a "country still fluctuating between the relics of former despotic dominion, and the liberal spirit of its present legislature."[32] To "enforce stability" in the British empire and in order for the administration to gain in "popularity," the "discouraged husbandman, the neglected artist, and oppressed laborer" would seek "asylum" in British "territories."[33] Print technology possessed all the rational and benevolent characteristics of the English government; the "vigour" and "impartiality" that marked the operations of the government were seen in the printed grammar book. Moreover, Halhed defines how the Bengali language was to be, and attempts to cleanse it, by doing away with "foreign" influences[34] and by presenting the Bengali language as "derived

---

[31] Ibid., p. xxv.

[32] Ibid., p. xvi.

[33] Ibid., p. xvi.

[34] Ibid., p. xx.

from its parent the Sanskrit";[35] words that were not "natives of the country are not a part of his text and he has only selected the "most authentic and ancient compositions."[36] The study of the language, Halhed argued, was made difficult due to the "carelessness and ignorance of the people"; it had many "anomalous characters" and deviations from the "original forms" giving rise to spurious characters.[37] The existing state of Bengali, as a language, was representative of the natives: lacking a sense of coherence and uniformity. Language and culture were imbued with the characteristics of a nation; the natives were emasculated and deviant, awaiting British colonization, akin to the fact that this scribal culture awaited print culture for progress. The spatial realm of the communications circuit mimicked and replicated the ideologies of the political.[38]

---

[35] Ibid., p. xxi.

[36] Ibid., p. xxii.

[37] Ibid., p. 3.

[38] Vidyasagar was to echo this criticism fifty years later.

Halhed was operating within existing Western ideologies where the British nation was construed as masculine in contrast to the effeminate colonies. Mrinalini Sinha makes a similar argument in *Colonial Masculinity: The "Manly Englishman" and the "Effeminate Bengali" in the Late Nineteenth Century*, when she states that the social constructs of the manly Englishman and the effeminate Bengali in nineteenth-century India were a result of the emerging dynamics between colonial and nationalist politics and "is best captured in the logic of colonial masculinity."[39] The contours of colonial masculinity were shaped in the context of an "imperial social formation that included both Britain and India."[40] The figures of the "manly Englishman" and the "effeminate Bengali *babu*," according to Sinha, "were produced by, and helped to shape, the shifts in the political economy of colonialism in the late nineteenth century."[41] Though Sinha

---

[39] Mrinalini Sinha, *Colonial Masculinity: The 'Manly Englishman' and the 'Effeminate Bengali' in the Late Nineteenth Century* (New York: St. Martin's Press, 1995), p. 1.

[40] Ibid., p. 2.

[41] Ibid., p. 3.

analyses nineteenth century colonial Bengal, the ideological contrasts of British masculinity and colonial effeminacy can be traced back to a hundred years ago, as Halhed makes clear.

There is nothing intrinsic to print for the technology to be considered as masculine and rational in comparison to manuscript texts. The characteristics of masculinity were socially ascribed to printed texts. In the early modern period in England, for example, writers were hesitant to see their works being printed, or to be seen ideologically and physically as involved in the marketplace of printers and publication. For the female writer, Jody Greene argues, publication was akin to prostitution, while the male writers shared this anxiety more acutely.[42] The act of publication, that is, submitting one's works to the press, made the writer vulnerable to charges of sexual deviance and indecent exposure. "The male writer," according to Wendy Wall, "always trades on his vulnerability when he agrees to play the female role and be

---

[42] Jody Greene, "Francis Kirkman's Counterfeit Authority: Autobiography, Subjectivity, Print," *PMLA* 121(1) 17-32.

'pressed' for the public."[43] By the seventeenth century, in England, increased literacy, the growth of cities and the flow of international capital improved print technology, and authors were more willing to make public works that would have a century ago been limited to private consumption. This caused an explosion in the number of printed books, doing away with how print was conceived. In eighteenth century England, print was seen at the apex of the communication system. For Halhed, writing in 1783, print was imbued with all the characteristics of the British nation and construed as vigorous, rational and truthful.

Scribal-manuscript culture, on the other hand, was defined as archaic and not very reliable. Halhed represents these elements of inauthenticity as inherent in the behavioural habits of the natives, stating that it was with "obstinate and inviolable obscurity the Jentoos conceal ... the Mysteries of their faith."[44] This

---

[43] Wendy Wall, *The Imprint of Gender: Authority and Publication in the English Renaissance* (Ithaca, Cornell UP, 1993), p. 182.

[44] Halhed, *A Grammar*, p. x.

particular grammar text, like other books printed by the scholar-administrators of the East India Company, would undo by making public the concealment, "obscurity" and archaic-ness of scribal knowledge. Halhed was engaged in revealing the knowledge systems that were "shut up in the libraries of Brahmins,"[45] and in undoing the "impenetrable reserve" of the Hindus.[46] While describing the efforts that were taken to write the grammar book, he says that he followed a very clear "set of rules" and in as "comprehensive" a manner as he could "devise" but the "task was rendered very laborious by the great multiplicity of observations" that he had collected.[47] For Halhed, modern print capitalism would give "a new fixity to language" allowing for a sense of "antiquity" of language" central to the formation of a modern consciousness.[48]

---

[45] Ibid., p. iii.

[46] Ibid., p. xi.

[47] Ibid., pp. xviii-xix.

[48] Benedict Anderson. *Imagined Communities. Imagined Communities: Reflections on the Origin and Spread of Nationalism* (New York: Verso, 1991), p. 44.

Therefore, the realm of print culture mimics the ideological realm of the political, making colonial rule possible.

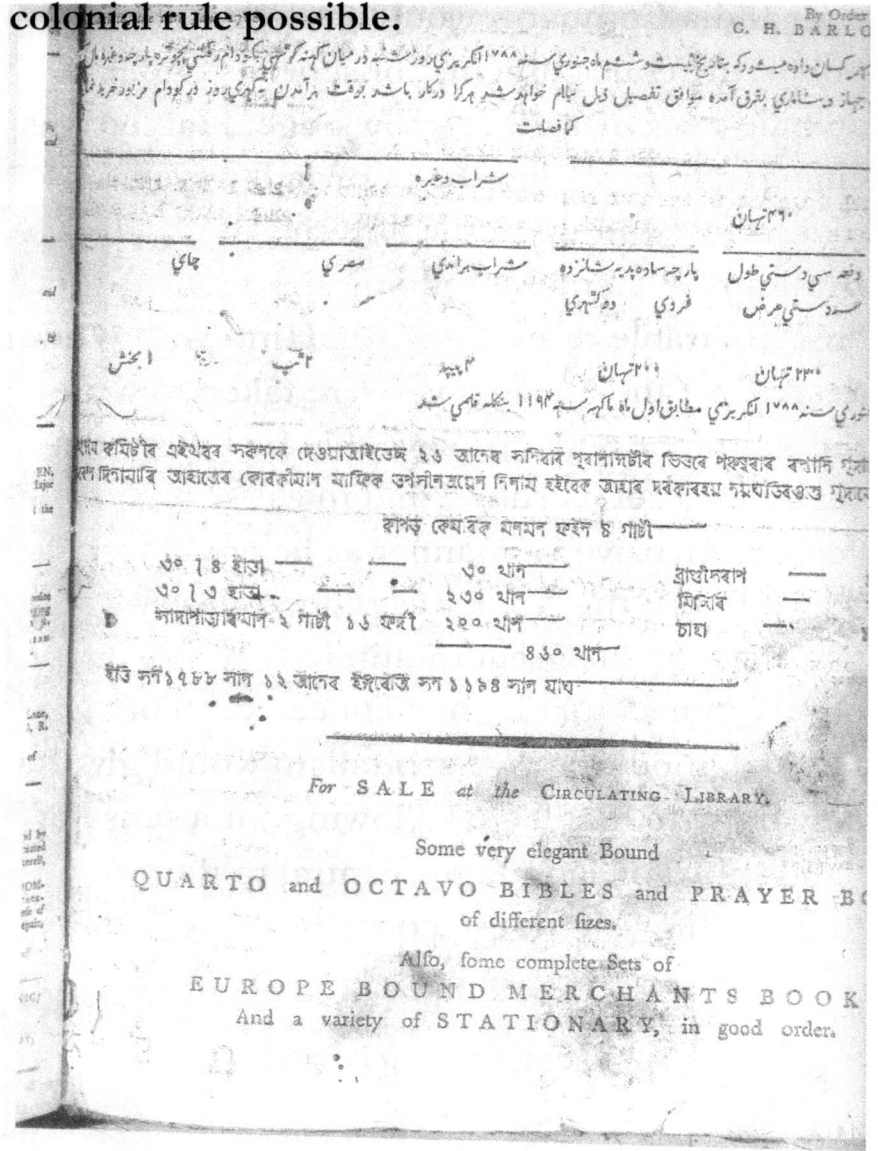

5 THE FIRST REALM OF PRINT

The early realm of print in Calcutta comprised of a wide variety of printed texts; from historical accounts like Francis Gladwin's *A dictionary of religious ceremonies of the eastern nations* (1787), William Hunter's *A Concise account of the kingdom of Pegu*,[49] to grammar books like John Gilchrist's *A dictionary, English and Hindoostanee*, and literary endeavors like *The bevy of Calcutta beauties. A collection of poems,*[50] *The poems of Anna Maria,*[51] *The happy prescription; or, the lady relieved from her lovers: a comedy in*

---

[49] Printed by John Hay, 1785.

[50] Published in Calcutta; printed by Daniel Stuart, 1785.

[51] Published in Calcutta: from the press of Thomson and Ferris, 1793.

rhyme.⁵² Official documents were also a part of this wide spectrum of printed material: like the East India Company *Treaties,*⁵³ Jonathan Duncan's *Bengal, Governor and Council. Translation of the regulations for the administration of justice in the Courts of Dewanny Adawlut*,⁵⁴ alongside historical narratives like Francis Gladwin's translation of Abu al-Fazl ib Mubarak's *Ayeen Akbery* and *The History of Hindostan, during the reigns of Jehangir, Shahejhan and Aurungzebe*.⁵⁵ Literary translations like *Kalidasa. The seasons: A descriptive poem, by Calidas, in the original Sanskrit,*⁵⁶ Joseph Champion's translations of *The Poems of Firdosi*,⁵⁷ medical treatises like Francis Balfour's *A treatise on the influence of the moon in fevers*,⁵⁸ travel narratives like Henry Abbott's *A journal with occasional*

---

[52] Written for a private theatre, by William Hayley, Esq. – Calcutta: printed in the year, 1785.

[53] Published in Calcutta: printed at the Honourable Company's Press, 1788.

[54] Printed at the Honourable Company's Press, 1784.

[55] From the press of Stuart and Cooper, 1788.

[56] Calcutta; printed at the Honourable Company's Press, 1792.

[57] Printed by John Hay, 1785.

[58] Printed by George Gordon, 1784.

remarks, made on a trip from Aleppo to Bussora[59] were also part of this large spectrum of printed texts.

The emergence of print culture in colonial Bengal, under the East India Company, is largely an untold story. Calcutta would become the capital of the British empire, and the realm of print culture played an important role in maintaining and perpetuating British rights to this colonial territory. The history of how this realm of print culture evolved in Calcutta is central focus here. Ships that sailed from England carried books; printing presses were brought all the way from Europe and with the help of Indians, print workshops were set up. Many fortune seekers who traveled to India in the hope of making money through printing ventures, set up printing presses and published newspapers. Sadly, many such ventures failed. Economic losses implied the absence of a readership. The focus was, unreasonably so, on being able to use print technology even when there was no

---

[59] From the press of Joseph Cooper, 1789

readership. Catalogues were published in Calcutta which advertised the books that had been imported from England which were auctioned on arrival like any other ships' cargoes. Printers mostly bought these imported books which were sold on to the public. Circulating libraries cropped up which needed imported books; an advertisement in the *Calcutta Gazette* in 1787 refers to the opening of a new library which stocked imported books: "Mr. Shakell [who succeeds John Hay as the printer of the *India Gazette*] having now arranged his late purchases by the last ships, and completed his Catalogue, presumes to assure the public that they will find his Circulating Library, well worthy of their patronage."[60] Tabloid-like gossip was also printed in newspapers. Oriental scholars had their works printed in Calcutta, the best known being Sir William Jones who also published journals on the proceedings of the Asiatic Society. Nonetheless, the reading public in Calcutta was small. In many ways, this realm of print enabled the community to imagine itself

---

[60] *Calcutta Gazette*, August 29, 1787.

to be a part of the British imperialist project, and bound it with the metropolis.

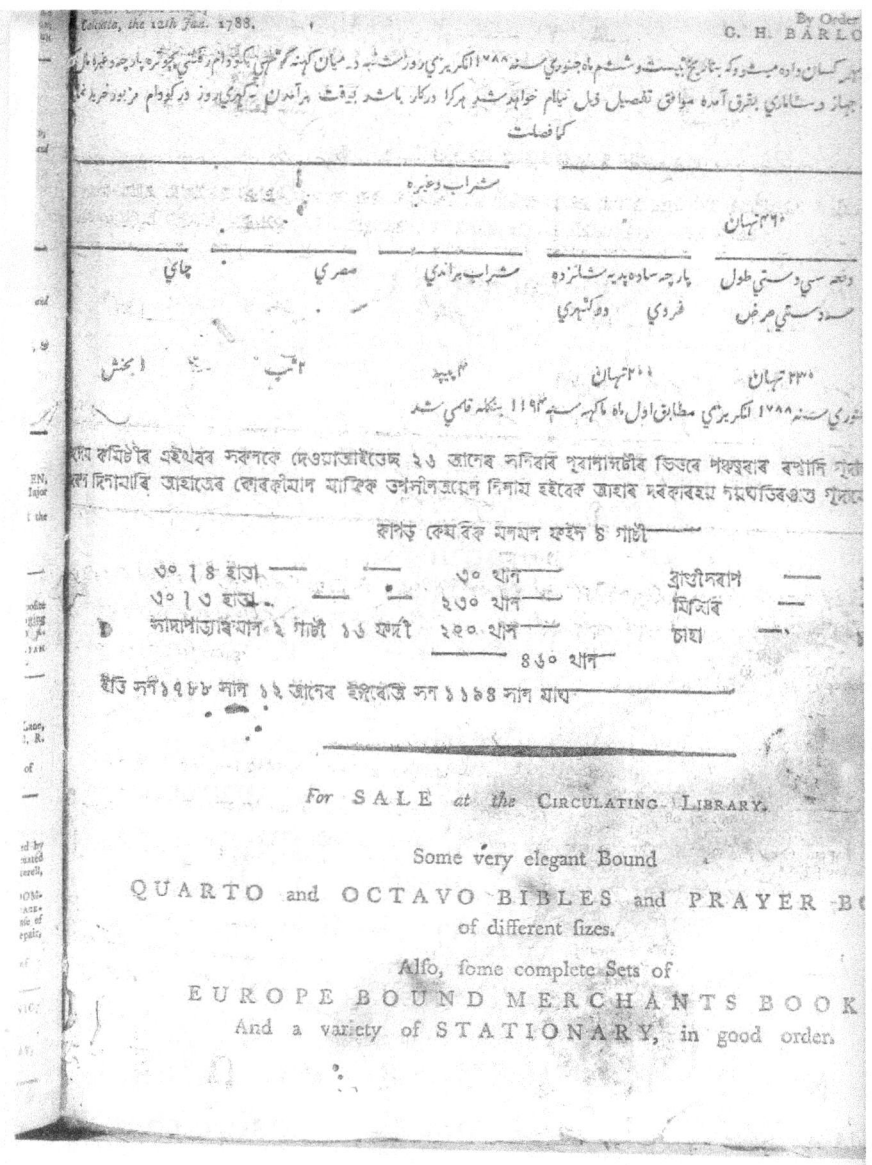

6 EAST INDIA COMPANY SPONSORED PRINT AND ORIENTALISM

The realm of print culture in Bengal was defined by the imperatives of empire; it would not have emerged the way it did if it had not been for the economic support of the East India Company. To clarify what I mean by imperial print, I examine the works of Sir William Jones and the Company Orientalists, a body of scholarship that emerged under the auspices of the East India Company. For Sir William Jones, steeped in the culture of print, the technology of print had the power to transform a pre-modern, Indian scribal culture into western modernity.

There was a sustained effort undertaken by the East India Company to ensure that there evolved a realm of print culture that contributed to imperial knowledge-making.

The process of imperial knowledge-making did operate outside a dichotomous relationship of European active observer and native passive observed, and recent scholarship draws attention to such a model of analysis. Imperial knowledge-making, in fact, involved both natives and British scholars. Sir William Jones, referred to as the father of scientific linguistics and comparative philology, is a perfect example of a scholar who worked outside the Orientalist knowledge-making framework. He was also steeped in the culture of eighteenth century British print and had an immense trust in the veracity of printed texts. An employee of the East India Company, Jones examined Indian languages in order to make linguistic connections with European languages, drawing attention to the complexities of the local culture while also placing it on a "pattern of human history at a global level."[61] In his annual address to the Asiatic Society in Calcutta, which he founded, in February 1789, Jones described the Sanskrit language within a global

---

[61] Kapil Raj. "Refashioning Civilites, Engineering Trust: William Jones, Indian Intermediaries and the Production of Reliable Legal Knowledge in Late Eighteenth Century Bengal," *Studies in History* 17(2001): 23-47, 29.

context, stating; that "the Sanskrit language, whatever be its antiquity, is of a wonderful structure; [it is] more perfect than the Greek, more copious than the Latin, and more exquisitely refined than either, yet bearing to both of them a stronger affinity."[62] Jones had a very clear idea of how the Asiatic Society would operate, revealing an awareness that the process of Company-sponsored Orientalist knowledge construction would have to involve the natives. Jones makes it clear when he says:

> Much may ... be expected from the communications of learned natives, whether lawyers, physicians, or private scholars, who should eagerly, on the first invitation, send us their ... [works] on a variety of subjects... . With a view to avail ourselves of this disposition, and to bring their latent science under our inspection, it might be advisable to print and circulate a short memorial, in Persian and Hindi ... [advertising] the design of our institution.

---

[62] William Jones, *The Collected Works of Sir William Jones. 3 Vols.* (New York: New York University Press, 1993), *Vol. 3*, p. 34.

> ... To instruct others is the prescribed duty of learned Brahmans, and, if they be men of substance, without reward; ... and the Mahomedans have not only the permission, but the positive commands, of their law giver, to search for learning even in the remotest parts of the globe.[63]

In his address to the white diasporic community in Calcutta comprising scholar-administrators, Sir William Jones encourages them to be involved in the apparatuses of knowledge-gathering, laying out specific instructions as to how they were to work. They were to "contribute a succinct description of such manuscripts" as had been "perused or inspected, with their dates and the names of their owners, and to propose for solution such questions as had occurred to him concerning Asiatik Art, Science, and History, natural or civil"; subsequently, the Asiatic Society would "possess without labour, ... a fuller catalogue of Oriental books."[54] It was through a

---

[63] Jones, *Collected Works, Vol. 3,* pp. 21-22.

[64] Ibid., pp. 21-22.

collaborative process, dependent on a relationship between the scholar and natives, that a catalogue of Oriental books could be established. Jones was implementing the strictures of British eighteenth century print culture, evident in his valorization of print technology as against manuscript culture.

The scholarship of Sir William Jones can be considered Company Orientalism and emerged only after 1780. Sanskrit, as a language, was till then, an enigma and remained elusive to Europeans. Sanskrit was seen as having the keys to a vast store of Indian knowledge, but there were very few who would help the Britishers learn the language. Most educated Hindus were hesitant to engage with Europeans and communicate to them any aspects of their own religion. But towards the end of the eighteenth century, with the rise of the East India Company as rulers, Orientalist scholarship as a disciplinary institution came into being under the patronage of the scholar-administrators of the Company. The East India Company substituted for native patronages of learning, and with the decline of the native aristocracies, many Brahmin scholars became destitute and gradually had to accept positions imparting knowledge to the new rulers.[65] For Sir William Jones, native scholars were to be used, but were never to be considered as intrinsic to the mission. For example, Jones wanted to admit natives into the Asiatic society but was unsure as to how his proposal would be received by the other Britishers. He compiled translations of Hindu and Muslim Laws in order to aid the "benevolent intentions of the legislature of Great Britain,"[66] using the knowledge of the "most learned Hindus and Mohammedans."[67] There was little "amusement" in working on these translations, except the belief and desire of "rendering his knowledge useful to his nation, and beneficial to the inhabitants of these provinces."[68] Company Orientalism, unlike Said's Foucault-inspired version of Orientalism, emerged as a

---

[65] Tony Ballantyne, *Orientalism and Race: Aryanism in the British Empire* (New York: Palgrave, 2002), pp. 1-55.

[66] Jones, *Complete Works, Vol. 3*, p. vi.

[67] Ibid., p. vii.

[68] Ibid., p. vii.

result of the close interaction between the natives and the Europeans and can be described as a detailed and organized body of knowledge fashioned by the East India Company in the late eighteenth century.[69]

The power of this realm of print culture is evident in the fact that it enabled to maintain control over the colonial territories. As early as 1783, a review appeared in an English journal, which when describing the need for grammar books and language books on the natives said that "without an easy and general intercourse with the natives, through the medium of language, no system of regulation … can promote any solid, rational or permanent establishment of authority and power" as no

---

[69] Central to Company Orientalism was a Sanskrito-centric vision of India that celebrated Sanskrit and the ancient past, but decried contemporary culture as debased. This attitude was in keeping with the eighteenth century fascination with the classical languages and literatures making the British believe that the ancient Hindus, like the Greeks and the Romans, had created a culture that was lost as a result of the medieval dark ages. Jones was much aware of the dichotomy within which he was operating, as he wrote, "Whoever travels in Asia, especially if he conversant with the literature of the countries through which he passes, must naturally remark on the superiority of European talents" (Jones, *Complete Works*, Vol. 3, p. 12). As "minute geographical knowledge "was needed" so was the knowledge of the "natural productions of these territories, especially in the vegetable and mineral systems" as these were "momentous objects of research to an imperial" and "commercial people" (Ibid., pp. 13-14).

people could "cheerfully submit to rulers" they did not understand."[70] More importantly, the cultivation of this kind of imperial print was a sustained effort and in keeping with the East India Company policies; the Company's trading success was a result of the scientific revolution of the seventeenth century and the EIC had eminent scientists of the Royal Society, like Robert Boyle, Isaac Newton, Joseph Banks as its directors or major shareholders. Not surprisingly, Company Orientalism had a small but influential readership, a sphere of print communication that informed the practices of empire formation.

---

[70] "Review of Halhed's Grammar Book," *The English Review, or, An Abstract of English and Foreign Literature* 1(1783): 5-14, 5.

7 SCRIBAL CULTURE

Empire making was made possible through the realm of print culture. Not only was the technology transferred, but so were the socially ascribed characteristics of print. Sir William Jones, operating within the ideology of eighteenth century print culture that associated print with truth, assumed that the technology of print had the power to transform a pre-modern, Indian scribal culture into western modernity. But this equation between print and truth was not intrinsic to letterpress technology as till the early decades of the eighteenth century there was a suspicion of the printed word. In *The Nature of the Book: Print and Knowledge in the Making*, Adrian Johns draws attention to assumptions about print culture, stating that what we "often regard as essential elements and necessary concomitants of print are in fact rather more contingent than generally acknowledged. Veracity in particular is … extrinsic to the press itself, and has had to be grafted onto it."⁷¹ A printed book could never be trusted to be what it claimed. Johns claims that in the seventeenth century, piracy and plagiarism were dominant fears. It was a matter of routine that books could be considered dubious; therefore, it was impossible to trust any printed report. Pirate editions of Shakespeare, Donne and Sir Thomas Browne were liable to egregious errors, and so was Sir Isaac Newton's unauthorized publication of *Principia* and the first scientific journal, the *Philosophical Transactions*. It was only in 1760 that the first book was printed without any errors.

Not surprisingly, till early in the eighteenth century, print was seen as suspect, without any intrinsic characteristic of truth.

---

[71] Adrian Johns, *The Nature of the Book: Print and Knowledge in the Making* (Chicago: University of Chicago Press, 2000), p. 2.

Printers, booksellers and authors, who gained the most commercially, put forward the notion of the truth and superiority of print in contrast to manuscripts. If print culture was to be a viable economical institution, a "communications circuit" involving the author, publisher, the printer, the shipper, the bookseller, and the reader had to be in harmonious coexistence, with the reader believing in the veracity of print. Writers were often propagandists of print, as much as theorists, and this is how Paula McDowell describes Daniel Defoe, the eighteenth century's "most prolific printed author," who wrote in his *Essay upon Literature* (1726), "The Printing Art has out-run the Pen, and may pass for the greatest improvement of its Kind in the World."[72] All of Defoe's writings imply that the oral past should be, but is not, cut off from the print-oriented present and future. Regarding Defoe's historical fiction, *A Journal of the Plague Year* (1772), McDowell points out that the text moves diachronically in time as the present modern

---

[72] Paula McDowell, "Defoe and the Contagion of the Oral: Modeling Media Shift in A Journal of the Plague Year," *PMLA* 121(1): 87-106.

age of print was a move away from the backward past associated with oral culture. Defoe also moves "synchronically across different communicative modes that in reality are coexisting and interdependent" but are represented as parts of a "linear, progressive development."[73] Defoe's printed books contribute to an "emergent model of a hierarchy of forms of communication with print at its apex"[74] as the writer attempts to draw an equation, not existing before, between print and "enhanced fidelity, reliability, and truth."[75] In this process, orality is relegated to the realm of old wives tales.

By the time of Sir William Jones, England had become an increasingly print-oriented society, shifting away from its oral past. This explains Jones' feverish desire to transcribe every manuscript into print, as the process would lend an element of fixity to unstable scribal texts. In an advertisement in *The*

---

[73] Ibid., p. 88.

[74] Ibid., p. 89.

[75] Johns, *The Nature of the Book*, p. 5.

Calcutta Gazette, in 1789, Sir William Jones wrote:

> The correctness of modern Arabian and Persian Books is truly deplorable, nothing can preserve them in any degree of accuracy but the art of printing; and if Asiatic literature should ever be general, it must diffuse itself, as Greek learning was diffused in Italy after the taking of Constantinople, by mere impressions of the best manuscripts without versions or comments, which future scholars would add at their leisure to future editions: but no printer should engage in so expensive a business without the patronage and the purse of monarchs of states, or society of wealthy individuals or at least without a large public subscription.[76]

Jones was extremely conscious of entering a

---

[76] William Jones, *The Calcutta Gazette*, October 29, 1789.

realm of scribal culture in Bengal, and this is reflected in his desire to constantly transfer manuscripts into printed texts. In a way, by transferring written texts into print, his central aim was to codify knowledge, and in the process allow for control of what was disseminated about India. In 1768, before Jones sailed for India, he wrote to Count Revicski, the Imperial Minister of Warsaw, describing the difficulties that were present when trying to locate a single meaning in manuscripts; it was "impossible to find two manuscripts [of Oriental literature] without error," he wrote, and "it was "absolutely necessary … to possess two copies of every one" which he would read so that "faults of the one" would be "corrected by the other."[77] In many of his letters, Jones voices a similar concern, where he reveals an intense desire to transcribe everything that he reads into print. Writing to one Dr. Patrick Russel in 1786, he said, "I congratulate you on the completion of your two works, but exhort you to publish them."[78] Jones goes on to say,

---

[77] Jones, *Complete Works, Vol. 1*, p. 101.

[78] Jones, *Complete Works, Vol. 2*, p. 99.

"think how much fame Koenig lost by delaying his publications" and even if printing is "dear at Calcutta," if "government" printed Russel's works, he would "cheerfully superintend commas and colons."[79] A year later, Jones voices a similar concern in another letter,

> I have just read a very old book on that art [of music] in Sanskrit. I hope to present the world with the substance of it, as soon as the transactions of our society [The Asiatic Society] can be printed; but we go slowly, since the press is often engaged by government; ... The *Asiatik Miscellany*, to which you allude, is not the publication of our society, who mean to print no scraps, nor any *mere* translations. It was the undertaking of a private gentleman, and will certainly be of use in diffusing Oriental literature, though it has [not?] been so correctly printed as I could wish.[80]

Manuscripts are seen as being less than perfect

---

[79] Ibid., pp. 100-101.

[80] Ibid., pp. 123-124.

while printed texts allow for true, correct knowledge to emerge. Print technology is invested with a kind of truth power that is denied to manuscripts. Power resides in the capacity to be able to use print, and in the process, to make it accessible to larger groups of people. Mechanical reproducibility, made possible as a result of letterpress technology, would make knowledge more reproducible but also more authentic. The realm of print spread across continents, and made it possible to control the colonial territories.

The East India Company was interested in documenting all forms of knowledge that it could lay its hands on and supported many such works; all grammar books and translations were justified as they could help in empire building. Translations of historical and administrative works were seen as essential in carrying out the operations of the Company, and often, these works were partially subscribed and recommended by the East India Company. For example, Francis Gladwin's translation of Abu al-Fazl Ibn Mubarak's *Ayeen Akbery* was published in

1783, and seen as an endeavor that would serve the company as the "work comprehends the original constitution of the Mogul Empire, described under the immediate inspection of its founder; and will serve to assist the judgment of the Court of Directors."[81] In the introduction to the translation, there is a lengthy explanation of how the text would be beneficial to the company: "It will show where the measures of their administration approach to the first principles, which perhaps will be found superior to any that have been built on their ruins, and certainly most easy, as the most familiar to the minds of the people, and when any deviation from them may be likely to counteract, or to assimilate with them."[82] The third volume contained a "full account of the religion of the Hindoos; their books and the subjects of them; their several sects and the points in which they differ."[83] There were

---

[81] *Ayeen Akbery: or The Institutes of the Emperor Akber*, Vol. I, trans. by Francis Gladwin, pp. xi-xii. 1783.

[82] Ibid., p. xi-xii.

[83] The "Preface" to *Ayeen Akbery*, Vol. III. trans. by Francis Gladwin. Printed by William Mackay, Calcutta Gazette Press, 1786.

astronomical notes which were provided by Reuben Burrow, who applied with "great diligence to the study of the Sanskrit language" and also made a "perfect knowledge of Hindoo astronomy."[84] The Governor General and Council recommended to the Court of Director the purchase of one hundred and fifty copies of the first edition of the *Ayeen Akbery*; this was, after all, a "work which may prove of the utmost utility to the Company, as it contains the original Institutes of the Sultan Akber, the founder of the empire."[85] Company patronage did provide a much needed monetary impetus for native types to be developed and these were subsequently used by the natives.

---

[84] Ibid.

[85] *Fort William-India House Correspondence, vol. IX, 1782-85*, edited by B.A. Saletore, Delhi, 1959. Also Gladwin's "Preface" to *Ayeen Akbery, Vol. II*, p. iii.

8 DIRT AND SQAULAOR AND PRINT

Did those Britishers who traveled to Calcutta towards the end of the eighteenth century arrive at a city that was extremely different from what they had left behind? In many ways, the dirt and squalor and the surrounding chaos of native life existed alongside the "white" city of Calcutta where there were beautiful, palatial houses and this was in some ways akin to what London was in the eighteenth century. By 1716, London was the largest European city and it was changing from a "compact traditional city to a rambling heterogeneous metropolis."[86] There was rapid migration, about 8,000 annually, of young people and women who were needed as servants and workers for

---

[86] *Walking the Streets of Eighteenth-century London, John Gay's Trivia (1716)*, eds. Clare Brant and Susan E Whyman, "Introduction." (New York: Oxford University Press, 2007), p. 4.

burgeoning industries, and these migrants settled in densely packed neighborhoods "marked by open sewers, decaying rubbish, virulent diseases and overflowing graveyards."[87] The streets were filled with the vulnerable part of the population, begging for a living and on the border of poverty. As Sophie Gee argues, that a "glut of waste matter fills the pages of eighteenth-century literature – not just in minority texts but in canonical works such as *Paradise Lost*, *The Tale of a Tub*, "A Modest Proposal," and *A Journal of the Plague Year*."[88] She goes on to write that this waste is "nothing if not memorable: Milton's infernal dregs, Swift's odious excrements, Pope's pissing contexts, Defoe's corpses."[89] At that time, this waste was supposed to be ignored but English writers were quite explicit in how waste was

---

[87] Ibid., p. 4.

[88] Sophie Gee, *Making Waste, Leftovers and the Eighteenth-Century Imagination* (Princeton: Princeton UP, 2009), pp. 2-3. In *Making Waste*, the first book about refuse and its place in Enlightenment literature and culture, Sophie Gee examines the meaning of waste at the moment when the early modern world was turning modern. Bernard Mandeville, praising English prosperity in *The Fable of the Bees*, told Londoners to treasure the dunghills in the streets, the running drains, animals, and crowds of beggars as daily reminders of London's wealth. p. 2-3.

[89] Ibid., p.3.

described in their literary works – "[d]ung, guts, and mud, dead dogs and turnip tops, sweep through the pages of eighteenth-century writing."[90] Maybe, in reality, it was not all that difficult for the Britishers to live in Calcutta, making us suspect their ramblings on how terrible life was in the colonial city. The following rant about hygiene and drinking water in a letter to the editor of a newspaper is truthful – undoubtedly, but while reading it, we do have to keep in mind that the conditions that they had left behind were really not that different.

As I was Jogging along in my Palanqueen yesterday, I could not avoid observing without a kind of secret concern for the health of several of my tender and delicate Friends, a String of Paria Dogs without an Ounce of Hair on some of them and in the last stage of the Meange plunge in and refresh themselves very comfortably in the great Tank – ... The great increase of Filth in it must

---

[90] Ibid., p. 2-3.

likewise add to its impurity and contribute not a little to give it that Raw disagreeable smell which is very perceptible upon a Comparative trial with other Waters."[91]

Ship loads of people arrived in Calcutta and they rebuilt a city and a social life that replicated what had been left behind in England; a republic of letters was formed and newspapers comprised a large part of this realm. Reading these texts give us a better understanding of the nature of their social life. There was an underlying premise that even if Calcutta was a colonial city inhabited with heathen natives, it was almost like living in a far away, newly established town which was beset with difficulties but was in the process of being made livable.

---

[91] *Bengal Gazette*, April 15th-22nd (1780): 2-3.

9 A WESTERNISED WHITE CITY IN CALCUTTA

At the end of the eighteenth century, the white population in Calcutta was quite small. In fact, part of the population was a migrant one and sailors comprised a large number. Often they stayed behind and joined the work force as there were ample job opportunities for poor white men. By the mid eighteenth century, there were European domestic servants, artisans and shopkeepers.[92] Builders, tailors, coachmakers, watchmakers, carvers set up their businesses employing Indian craftsmen; dancing and music teachers held classes for members of the rich community and Calcutta was known as a "settlement dominated by

---

[92] P.J. Marshall. "The White Town of Calcutta under the Rule of the East India Company," *Modern Asian Studies* 34.2 (May): 307-331; pp. 309-310.

wealthy men who lived high."[93]

The white elite of Calcutta prided themselves on having created in India an environment in which the best of contemporary British institutions were faithfully reproduced. …. White Calcutta under the Company was a remarkably British place. … Its development was largely unplanned and its main services, such as drainage, roads and police, were of a low standard. But it had individual buildings of considerable ambition … and its wealthy citizens enjoyed many amenities: books, theatre, music and learned societies.[94]

The city developed in a haphazard manner. The municipal services of the city which were provided by the Company were not in good shape. European architects designed houses

---

[93] Ibid., p. 312.

[94] Ibid., p. 328.

that were built in grand, classical styles and not suited for the climate.[95] Churches, schools and orphanages were also built. The prospects of making a fortune were very bright. Banking and trading houses were set up.[96] Apart from those who were directly employed by the East India Company, there grew a class of rich white elites who were involved in different capacities with the numerous civic institutions that cropped up: "partners in the private banks, insurance companies and the ubiquitous agency houses, ... which managed shipping, indigo factories and a wide range of [trading] activities."[97] By 1769, the East India Company had started to implement British laws. With the establishment of the Supreme Court in 1774 that dealt with litigation involving both the Europeans and Indians, lawyers were able to reap enormous profits.

---

[95] Ibid., p. 316.

[96] Ibid., pp. 310-318.

[97] Ibid., p. 313.

10 BOOK ADVERTISEMENTS AND PRINT

No eighteenth-century book in England emerged from the printer without "pages of advertisements, printed or pasted onto the back," thus allowing for print to promote print.[98] Consumer fetishism was not limited to the use of material things, and a similar desire is evident in how printed texts were published and consumed in Calcutta. The advertisements in the newspapers allow us to gauge the nature of the communication network between author, reader, printer, and publisher that was evident in Calcutta. The newspapers and books that were printed in Calcutta, based on subscription readership, ensured the printers a sense of

---

[98] Barbara Benedict, *Readers, Writers, Reviewers and the Professionalization of Literature* (Cambridge: Cambridge University Press, 2006), p. 7.

economic viability. This model of subscription publication was a system in use in eighteenth century England. Till the seventeenth century, there had been censorship in England, allowing the government control and surveillance of the kinds of books that were printed, and the number of books that could be printed. With the lapse of the Licensing Act in 1695, a free sphere of print culture evolved, without systematic government intervention. John Brewer describes the emergence of this realm of eighteenth century printers and publishers.[99] In 1689, the world of printing was limited to a few sections of London in St. Paul's Churchyard and Paternoster Row, dominated by a powerful trade guild, and was a community where everyone knew everybody else. But a hundred years later, the publishing industry had grown and in 1785, John Pendred wrote the first guide to English publishing which covered the provinces: *The London and Country Printers, Booksellers and Stationers Vade Mecum.* What "had begun as a London

---

[99] John Brewer, "Authors, Publishers and the Making of Literary Culture," in *The Book History Reader,* ed. David Finkelstein and Alistair McCleery (London and New York: Routledge, 2002).

trade had become a national business."[100] The rise of the periodical press made it possible for the professional writer to emerge, and have a career based solely on writing. Commercial publishing meant the bookseller had the upper hand in determining what kinds of books were to be printed, displayed, and were sales-worthy. Subscription made it possible for the inevitable commercial viability in the market place, and the independence of the author as it implied a certain amount of sales, which covered production and distribution costs. The eighteenth century saw subscription publication emerge, bringing together the interests of the author, patron and bookseller. The subscriber had become the patron—which in the earlier centuries was the role played by the Court or wealthy individuals. This model was followed by the printers and writers in Calcutta, and ensured some degree of economic independence for emergent writers.

With the emergence of subscription readership the relationship between the author,

---

[100] Ibid., p. 244.

reader and printer changed. Newspapers played a role in disseminating news about new publishing ventures, becoming a medium though which new printing enterprises were advertised and therefore, it was through print that a desire for more print was created and sustained. For example, an advertisement for a new weekly publication, the *Chittagong Herald,* was announced in the following manner in the *Calcutta Chronicle*: "Three gentlemen have stepped forward in support of this agreeable 'Publication' and look forward to entertain their 'small settlement' every Sunday." A poem was enclosed, addressed to the Public: "Ye gentlemen and ladies all, / Who live at Chittagong, / On you the Herald means to call / Each Sunday, with a song;" and the poem ends with a few lines from the printer, "Great-Sir, I beg you'll tell the town, / My types are very few; / My press is old and broken down, / With scarce a single screw."[101] By informing the readers of new literary and journalistic ventures, and also by often making requests for monetary advances, a subscription-based

---

[101] *Calcutta Chronicle*, March 13 (1792): 4.

readership was formed.

It is fascinating to examine the nature of the books that were printed and sold by the printers in Calcutta; advertisements reveal the specific nature of what was being printed:[102] *History of the Bible and Catechetical Instruction with a Persian Translation, Sold for the Benefit of the Protestant Mission in Bengal*. Grammar books were written in volumes: "Gilchrist's *Grammar*, Chapter III, is now ready for Delivery, at the Chronicle Office, to such Subscribers who send for it. The Fourth Chapter will be published shortly, due Notice will be given." The printers served as book sellers, and there was an absence of a separate establishment for books to be published. There were advertisements for books that were to be published, and waited for buyers; "Speedily will be published an edition of *Angelo's School of Fencing, with a General Explanation of the Principal Attitudes and Positions Peculiar to the Art*. [it is only on request] – Those gentlemen who are inclined to favor the

---

[102] *Calcutta Chronicle*, April 3 (1792): 3.

publication will be pleased to signify their intentions to Mr. Upjohn." Often, these proposals would be in addition to lengthy descriptions of the text that was to be printed:[103] "Proposals for Publishing by Subscription, *The Musical Olio, or Chearful Companion: Being A Collection of Songs, sung at The Anacreontick Society, The Beef-Steak Club, and Several Other Convivial Meetings*; by Dibdin and Others. The Work to be printed on English Foolscap, with a beautiful Type; to consist of One Hundred and Fifty Pages, and to contain near Two Hundred Songs,—When Fifty copies are subscribed for, the Work will be put to Press. And it is the Compiler's Intention to Print off no more than are really subscribed for. Gentlemen wishing to become Subscribers to the above Work will be pleased to make known their intentions to Mr. A. B. Bone, at the Circulating Library." Thus, the realm of printed texts—of grammar books, translations, poems—that emerged in the last two decades of the eighteenth century in Calcutta catered to the needs of the Britishers.

---

[103] *Calcutta Chronicle*, Nov. 6 (1792).

11 MULTILINGUAL TEXTS

Between 1780 and 1800, many newspapers in Calcutta printed news in multiple languages side by side on the same sheet of paper. This was a moment in the history of newspapers in England and in India that had not happened before and was not replicated subsequently. Any reader of these beautiful multilingual sheets of paper would question as to why such newspapers went out of fashion in a few decades after they were printed. Not only had the new technology of print culture entered India with the Britishers but also, this technology, in the process of establishing itself within a colonial situation, underwent changes on how it was conceptualized. Colonization determined the nature of print culture which is why multilingual newspapers emerged in Calcutta and for a few moments in the history of print culture and of newspapers, there were such heteroglossic texts. The sheer new-ness of the visual text was and is mind-boggling in all respects – specially if we see how radical it was conceptually.

    Is it possible that such a multilingual text could only happen in south Asia where a multilingual society exists. In some ways, and unwittingly so, the Britishers captured an aspect of Indian society within these printed texts and the sheer spirit of invention marks these newspapers. The possibilities of what could have been if newspapers had continued to be multilingual are not explored for it denotes an epistemic shift, thus answering a question: what happens when a technology that has its origins in a different social space enters a new geographical locale and how does it change? The heteroglossic nature of Indian society was reflected in how these newspapers were formed; moreover, in some ways, the Britishers were attempting to portray and capture Indian society in these newspapers.

What remains a fuzzy unexplored area is whether the natives took up print culture easily enough or was there initial resistance at the advent of the new technology? The nature of print that entered south Asia had evolved since its beginnings three hundred years ago in the west. Even a hundred years ago, there was conflicting attitudes in England towards print technology. Manuscript culture was present even after 1710 and the Act of Queen Anne and it was considered a "competitive if not the dominant mode of transmitting and reading 'literary' and 'academic' materials."[104] This act of clinging on to an "outdated" technology of the fading aristocratic world of letter represented an authorial choice. But obviously enough, there were enormous epistemic shifts made as a result of print and Eisenstein writes about its revolutionary impact on how science was conceptualized:

> The advantages of issuing identical images bearing identical labels to

---

[104] Margaret Ezell, *Social Authorship and the Advent of Print*, Baltimore (John Hopkins University Press, 2003), p. 12.

scattered observers who could feed back
information to publishers enabled
astronomers, geographers, botanists, and
zoologists to expand data pools far
beyond all pervious limits – even those set
by the exceptional resources of the long
lasting Alexandrian Museum. ... The
closed world of the ancients was opened;
vast expanses of space (and later of time)
previously associated with divine
mysteries became subject to human
calculation and exploration.[105]

As a result of print, knowledge could spread in faster methods than had been possible previously. In the western world, the shift that took place from a manuscript culture was a gradual but inevitable one, but we do not really such ambiguities in how print culture was perceived by the natives in Calcutta as the sophisticated social characteristics of late eighteenth century print were transferred on to the colony. In Bengal, the Britishers developed native fonts, which were subsequently made

---

[105] Eisenstein, pp. 256-257.

use of by the natives. But, did the availability of fonts make it easier for the natives to make the shift from manuscript to print culture? More importantly and is a question we should be asking at the present is whether native usage was impacted by the fact that the Britishers made use of native fonts? In what can but only be described as being ironical, the Britishers printed multilingual texts but these were subsequently used in a different context altogether by the natives. These texts that were initially printed by the Britishers for their own needs, incidentally represented the multilingual nature of Indian society.

The efforts that were taken to obtain and create fonts and types in Indian languages are little known facts. Many of the newspapers would be beautifully illustrated with Indian languages and a single page would have Urdu, and Bengali side by side. During the time period that I am referring to - between 1780 and 1820 - these newspapers were only read by the Britishers, which means that the Indian languages only had English readers. In 1830, a report in *The Friend of India* said that before this period, "the press had been confined to Europeans, and the only works in the native languages were printed at their expense and circulated gratis."[106] A question that needs to be answered is: why were there elaborate Indian prints in newspapers that would not necessarily be read by all the English readers of the newspapers?

The larger argument that was used to legitimate British colonization was that it was needed to do good for the natives; this explains to a great extent many of the socio-cultural and technological exchanges that took place between the Britishers and the natives. The relationship is best described in the following manner:

Britain possesses the means of improvement and instruction beyond most nations in Europe. India on the contrary is ignorant and wretched, while a bounteous Providence is pouring forth

---

[106] "Art. V. - On the effect of the Native Press in India," *The Friend of India*. Quarterly Series (No. 1): 130-154, p. 133.

upon her almost every blessing which can render a country happy. But it is to Britain alone that she can look for instruction and relief. Did other nations posses the means of imparting them in the fullest manner, the opportunity is denied them. How could any other nation interfere so as to gain the confidence of India? It is to Britain alone that Providence has committed this pleasing task, and in a more full and ample manner than has ever been done to any nation at any former period.[107]

The reason that was used to justify the need for colonization was that the Indians needed the Britishers for "improvement and instruction" because as a nation, Britain alone could provide them with the required education as the other nations "lacked" the means of imparting them. Moreover, during the early years of British presence, the task of colonization was seen as a "pleasing" one which would enable the Indians

---

[107] Ibid., p. 135.

to "gain the[ir] confidence." It would be a meaningful enterprise if we allowed ourselves to view print culture as part of the process of "instruction" accompanying empire and colonization. This implies that we have to consider print as functioning against manuscript culture and regard it as it was considered by the Britishers: a vast systemic and civilizational improvement.

It was not only that print technology symbolized the British colonizers desire to promote the arts of peace but there were some necessary practical reasons to why such heteroglossic texts were printed and circulated amongst the white community. Francis Gladwin, wrote in a letter in 1784 to the Board of Directors of the EIC as to why a newspaper like *The Calcutta gazette, or Oriental Advertiser* was needed; "[to start a gazette] as it might be made Useful to the Junior part of the Company's Servants by the insertion of Extracts from the most approved Persian Authors; in the original Character with English Translations, and thus facilitate their Improvement in that Language, the study of which has been so frequently recommended to them by the Court of Directors."[108] In the preface to the *Asiatik Miscellany*, Gladwin wrote that it would be an enterprising endeavor to print Persian works alongside English translations:

> And though this part of the Work may, at first sight, seem particularly designed for those who study the Persian language, and will undoubtedly be of singular use to them, it is yet by no means on their account alone, that the extracts appear in that form. The translations will, we trust, be always matter of curiosity and entertainment to English readers also, who in seeing them accompanied by their respective originals, will have no reason to be satisfied, that what is presented to them as a specimen of eastern history or composition, is neither spurious nor disguised by borrowed ornament, but is genuine, pure and unadulterated.[109]

---

[108] Quoted in *A History of the Calcutta Press*, Nair, p. 110.

[109] Quoted in Ibid., pp. 116-117.

British superiority was evident in that print could erase the impure and adulterated parts of a manuscript language. The natives must have accepted this assumption for we find scant criticism against the emergence of native types and print.

12 CAN UTILITARIANISM MAKE THE NATIVES HAPPY?

India, as a colony, was viewed as a precious possession and such a view is articulated quite strongly in a text like *The Annals of the College of Fort William*,[110] which was written in the early nineteenth century and symptomizes some of the basic principles underlying empire formation: the empire should be maintained with the "spirit of enterprise and boldness which acquired it" but it should not "be administered as a temporary and precarious acquisition -- as an Empire conquered by prosperous adventure, and extended by fortunate accident, of which the tenure is as

---

[110] *The Annals of the College of Fort William. from the Period of its Foundation.* Arranged and Published by Thomas Roebuck, Calcutta (Printed by Philip Periera at the Hindoostanee Press, 1819), pp. i-iii.

uncertain as the original conquest and successive extension were extraordinary"; the colony would be considered "as a sacred trust, and a permanent succession."[111] Notwithstanding such a view about the colony, there is still no direct reason as to why there was a need to invest so much intellectual resources into India and what determined the underlying principles behind colonization? But we do find that there are abstract concepts of goodness and happiness that recur over and over again in a text like *The Annals of the College of Fort William*, which nudge us towards assuming, that at least, during the initial years of empire building in India, British imperialism did desire to portray itself as something more than mere brute power. The assumption that the act of colonization would lead to the happiness of the natives is clearly an utilitarian one and is best summarized in John Stuart Mill's definition of Utilitarianism when he described it as that "creed which accepts as the foundation of morals, Utility, or the Greatest Happiness Principle, holds that

---

[111] Ibid., p. xi.

actions are right in proportion as they tend to promote happiness, wrong as they tend to produce the reverse of happiness."[112] In the "Introduction" to the *Annals*, which mostly puts forward a rationale of the newly established College of Fort William, the English readers are told that the "general happiness and prosperity of the country" depended on the "conduct" of the civil servants of the EIC, and they would be unable to engage in communication unless they were conversant with the "Native languages" and the laws and customs of the land.[113] It was the "sacred duty, true interest, honour and policy of the British nation" that compelled the British government to rule for the "prosperity and happiness" of the people of India.[114] In a similar manner, it was argued that the English would preserve Indian culture in a more comprehensive fashion than had been, and therefore the need to preserve manuscripts was that it would eventually lead to the happiness of the Indians:

---

[112] Stuart Mill, *Utilitarianism* (London: Longmans, Green, Reader and Dyer, 1871), pp. 9-10.

[113] *Annals*, p. iii-iv.

[114] Ibid., p. xv.

The preservation and augmentation of the Collection of Eastern Manuscripts, afford the only means of arresting the progressive destruction of Oriental learning. Since the dismemberment of the Muslim, those works have been dispersed over India, and have been exposed to the injuries and hazards of time, accident and neglect. It is worthy of the ambition of this great Empire to employ every effort of its influence in preserving from destruction and decay, these valuable records of Oriental history, Science and Religion.[115]

By engaging with the natives and by teaching them, the Indian subjects would also have a more favourable view of the British rulers. There would diffuse among them "a spirit of civilization and an improved sense of those genuine principles of morality and virtue," that

---

[115] Ibid., p. 114.

would promote their happiness and establish a stable British empire.[116]

The civil servants were not the "agents of a commercial concern" but were the "ministers and officers of a Powerful Sovereign."[117] Their education in the College of Fort William would help them to discharge their duties in a manner that would allow them to "honour" the "British name in India" and would lead to the "prosperity and happiness" of the "Native subjects."[118] They would learn to perform the duty of ruling "the extensive and valuable dominions" the nation had acquired in India, for by discharging this duty, depended the "prosperity and permanency" of the Empire.[119] The education of the civil servants would not be exclusively "European or Indian" but would involve the combined principles of Asian and European policy and government." Their education would be of a mixed nature, the

---

[116] Ibid., p. 115

[117] Ibid. p. iv.

[118] Ibid., p. v.

[119] Ibid., p.19.

"foundation" laid in England and "the superstructure systematically completed in India."[120] The College of Fort William was meant to teach the civil servants so that they could understand the existing laws and regulations, thus "enabling" them to discharge their duty.[121] Good administration would eventually create happy subjects:

> The due administration of just laws within these flourishing and populous provinces, is not only the foundation of the happiness of millions of people, but the main pillar of the vast fabric of the British Empire in Asia; the mainspring of our Empire is situated here…
>
> … the excellence of the general spirit of these laws is attested by the noblest proof of just, wise, and honest government; by the restoration of happiness, tranquility, and security, to an oppressed and suffering people, and by the revival of agriculture, commerce, manufacture, and

---

[120] Ibid., p. xii.

[121] Ibid., p. 92.

general opulence in a declining and impoverished country.[122]

The fundamental premise was that the natives would welcome British presence and would want to be ruled and such an explanation partially explains the enormous flow of culture and technology into India. It is within this Utilitarian interpretative model that we can understand the enormous efforts taken to not only create native fonts, but also the need to set up the institution of print culture in an elaborate manner.

---

[122] Ibid., pp. 93-94.

13 HOW NATIVE FONTS WERE MADE

In a succinct commentary on how it took centuries for print to develop in the west, unlike the rapid manner in how it evolved in Calcutta, Halhed, in *The Grammar of the Bengal Language*, summarizes the efforts taken by Charles Wilkins to perfect the native types:

> With a rapidity unknown in Europe, he surmounted all the obstacles which necessarily clog the first rudiments of a difficult art, as well as the disadvantages of solitary experiment; and has thus singly on the first effort exhibited his work in a state of perfection which in every part of the world has appeared to require the united the united improvements of

different projectors, and the gradual polish of successive ages.[123]

When the East India Company government established its printing press, Wilkins was its first head. But as we look closely at the nitty gritty details of the workings of the Srirampur Mission Press, one realizes that natives were active participants in the process of how technology was exchanged; Joshua Marshman, while describing Panchanan's efforts, wrote: "[with his] assistance we created a letter foundry, and although he is dead now, he had so full communicated his art to a number of others, that they carry forward the work of type casting, and even of cutting the matrices with a degree of accuracy which would not disgrace European artists."[124] Largely due to the efforts of William Carey, there was interaction between the Srirampur Mission press and the College of Fort William and many of the books written by

---

[123] Halhed, pp. xxiii-xxiv.

[124] From Sisir Kumar Das' *Sahibs and munshis: an account of the College of Fort William* (Calcutta: Orion Publications, 1978), p. 96.

the scholars of the college were printed in this press. Carey appointed many good scribes in different languages. The Bengali letters were engraved on the basis of a sample prepared by Kali Kumar Ray, the Bengali copyist of the College. Kali Kumar Ray must have been a scribe. What is interesting is that both natives and Englishmen were involved in the process of making types, therefore making the evolution of Indian print a collaborative venture.[125]

Panchanan taught the art of cutting types to Manohar, who was to become his son in law. Marshman described Manohar as "an expert and elegant workman who was subsequently employed for forty years at the Srirampur Press and to whose exertions and instructions Bengal is indebted for the various beautiful fonts of the Bengali, Nagree, Persian, Arabic and other characters which have been gradually introduced into the different printing

---

[125] *Annals:* "Many learned Natives are now attached to the Institution, who have been invited to Fort William by my special authority from different parts of Asia. … The sudden dismission of the learned Natives attached to the College would therefore be an act of manifest injustice on the grounds already stated; it would also be an act of the most flagrant impolicy; nor would it be consistent either with the interest or the honour of the Company in India, …pp. l-li.

establishments."[126] Over a span of around thirty years, between 1801-1830, the Srirampur Mission press printed books in over fifty languages.

A lot of intellectual labor went into the process of making types and perfecting the font. John Gilchrist made some changes to the printing of the Perso-Arabic scripts. In 1802, he wrote to the College Council: "as the types and printing materials which Mr. Gladwin presented to College are probably the best now to be procured, I request you will state to College my wish to take charge of, and employ them for the good of my department here, in the works I am about to publish in Hindoostanee language."[127] He also promised to return the types when needed to the College Council and thus was started the Hindoostane Press. Till then, there were some presses in operation: the Chronicle Press, Stuart and Cooper Press, Ferris and Greenway Press, and

---

[126] From *Sahibs and munshis*, p. 97.

[127] Ibid., p. 98.

the Hurkaru Press. On 20th June, Gilchirst wrote to the College Council that he had made major improvements in 'Oriental typography' on the "European principle of separating words by spaces and joining the letters of each vocable, as much as possible." Lumsden subsequently made changes to Gilchrist's innovations. In 1805, he presented plans of improving the existing types in Persian and for establishing a new press. He also wanted a new set Persian types to be made by the best artists in Calcutta, under the guidance of Sheikh Kutb Ali, the Persian writing master at the College. He argued that "the letters of the Persian alphabet are joined together in such a manner as to render the frequent use of Logographic types indispensably necessary to the accurate execution of any literary work that may be printed in the Persian character."[128] The types that were used by the College were meant to "imitate more nearly the written character" and it was hoped that the printed texts would vie with "manuscripts in beauty and cheapness" even as they surpassed manuscripts in

---

[128] Ibid., p. 99.

"accuracy."[129] The types were executed under the immediate supervision of natives attached to the College.[130]

It is not surprising that there are detailed discussions on the painstaking efforts taken to create the new types of Indian languages, and the sheer beauty of these native mechanical fonts. The emphasis was on the mechanical superiority of print versus handwritten manuscripts and to understand the logic of this argument, one needs to remember that by the end of the eighteenth century, when the socio-cultural characteristics of print were carried alongside the technology of print itself, print culture was seen at the apex of the communication circuit in Europe. Print technology in Europe during the fifteenth and sixteenth centuries reflected the larger social shift that was taking place whereby handicraft productions were giving way to mechanical processes and scribes were being replaced. For this change to occur, a fundamental shift had to

---

[129] *Annals*, p. 210.

[130] Ibid., p. 211.

take place where printed books were construed as more credible than manuscripts; printers thus started to champion the superior accuracy and credibility of books in comparison to manuscripts at the beginning of the sixteenth century.[131] There was nothing intrinsic to the trustworthiness of books, and in fact, Adrian Johns argues that when printed books were first published in the early modern period, textual corruptions multiplied but this time period also saw the social constructedness of printed texts as being fixed and credible in comparison to handwritten texts.[132]

Within the colonial context in Calcutta, when we look closely at the debates and rationale raised on how the realm of print was to emerge, the concerns were not merely with replacing a manuscript culture, but there was an equally strong emphasis on how beautiful the natives types were. Halhed, in the "Introduction" to the *Grammar of the Bengal*

---

[131] Johns, 1998, p. 5.

[132] Ibid., p.31.

Language wrote on the mechanical aspects of the fonts:

> The public curiosity must be strongly excited by the beautiful characters which are displayed in the following work: and although my attempt may be deemed incompleat or unworthy of notice, the book itself will always bear an intrinsic value, from its containing as extraordinary an influence of mechanic abilities as has perhaps ever appeared. That the Bengal letter is very difficult to be imitated in steel will readily be allowed by every person who shall examine the intricacies of the strokes, the unequal length and size of the characters, and the variety of their positions and combinations. It was no easy task to procure a writer accurate enough to prepare an alphabet of a similar and proportionate body throughout, and with that symmetrical exactness which is necessary to the regularity and neatness of a fount.[133]

---

[133] Halhed, p. xxiii.

The element of beauty involved in the creation of the types in Indian languages is a factor that has never been considered in how print was construed in Europe. In many ways, such a perspective compels us to be more nuanced in how empire worked in the colonial context, legitimizing the need to invest time, labour, money and people in establishing a realm of print.

14 NATIVE MASTERY

The realm of early nineteenth century print culture in Calcutta was a heterogeneous space: Europeans printing books for themselves for reasons of politics, administration, aesthetics, proselytization and natives learning about this realm through close interaction. The picture that emerges is one of constant activity where natives and colonizer engaged with print in a heteroglossic manner.[134] A similar perspective allow us to state that when we try to draw a

---

[134] Such an inclusive perspective in the socio-literary history of print is argued for by Robert Darnton in his essay, "The Forgotten Middlemen of Literature," where Robert Darnton argues that the communication circuit does not necessarily only include books; some "unfamiliar figures" have to be added -- like the "rag pickers, papermakers, typesetters, wagon drivers, booksellers, and even readers." Darnton argues that our knowledge of literary history has to be more inclusive and we would take into account the everyday lives of men and women "who had a way with words." In *The Kiss of Lamourette. Reflections in Cultural History* (New York: Norton, 1990).

picture of the early years of English literary writings in Calcutta, and the use of print by these writers, we are compelled to make certain assumptions in the absence of any concrete anecdotes of what was happening. My specific focus in this section is on Henry Derozio who was writing in the early years of the nineteenth century and is considered as the first Indian poet writing in English.[135] Here, I argue that he was able to engage with print and English literary conventions with reasonable sophistication that was not possible for most natives at that time, because of his social and racial positional -- more *sahib* than native. It is due to the efforts of writers like Derozio that natives subsequently engaged with the realm of English literature. Derozio was an outsider of sorts and despite that was able to consider the English literary tradition as his own. This would have encouraged newly anglicized young natives to do the same.

---

[135] All works of Derozio are cited from the following collection, *Derozio, Poet of India. The Definitive Edition.* edited by Rosinka Chaudhuri (Calcutta: Oxford University Press, 2008).

Derozio is considered as the first Indian to write English poetry. This is a bit random - was he Indian after all? As an East Indian, Derozio identified himself as an Indian, yet he was culturally and racially more *sahib* than native Indian. There are numerous poems and essays in the literary journals that were printed in the last two decades of the eighteenth century and early years of the nineteenth century. They were all written in India, for an Indian readership, but for a readership that was mostly British and lived in India for reasons of work. The institution of print was Indian, except the readership. This sphere of print was replicated and learnt by the natives. This is the context which we have to use in order to understand Derozio. We also have to keep in mind that English literature was going to influence all spheres of Indian literature. Pierre Bourdieu[136] aptly describes this phenomenon of "cultural production" where English literary writings would dominate the native scenario as the "site of struggle" when what was at "stake" was the

---

[136] Pierre Bourdieu, "The Field of Cultural Production," in *The Book History Reader*, eds. David Finkelstein and Alistair McCleery (New York: Routledge, 2002), pp. 77-99.

power to "impose the dominant definition of the writer" and in the process "delimit the population of those entitled to take part in the struggle to define the writer";[137] Derozio was participating in and defining what would become the dominant definition of literature in India. Henry Derozio published his first collection called *Poems* in 1827; the Baptist Mission Press was his publishing house. The same press published one of Rammohun Roy's initial works in 1819, *A Second Conference Between an Advocate and an Opponent on the Practice of Burning Widows Alive.* Everybody in the domain of English print knew each other. It was, after all, a small realm of print.

We will never know for sure if the multilingual newspaper, in some way, indicates the Britishers desire to engage with India to a greater extent than was needed, but there is reason to believe so as in the early decades of the nineteenth century, there were debates regarding the possibility of Europeans settling in India which would have given them the

---

[137] Ibid., pp. 77-79.

impetus to learn native languages. We know that there was a dialogue regarding this issue as Rammohun Roy wrote a tract titled, "Remarks on Settlement in India by Europeans"[138] where he describes these debates: "Much has been said and written by persons in the employ of the Hon. East India Company and others on the subject of the settlement of Europeans in India, and many various opinions have been expressed as to the advantages and disadvantages which might attend such a political measure." Rammohun Roy was a cultural mediator for the Britishers, explaining Indian customs to the rulers, and the theme of European settlement features in Rammohun's writings. That Rammohun did deal with such a social issue is surprising but indicates that it must have been under consideration to a certain degree, and draws attention to the heterogeneity of Indian society.

Rammohun begins his analysis in by locating his own position as an employee of the

---

[138] Rammohun Roy, "Remarks on Settlement in India by Europeans." in *The English Works of Raja Rammohun Roy. Part III*, (eds.) Kalidasa Nag and Debajyoti Burman (Calcutta, Sadharon Brahmo Samaj), pp. 79-86.

East India Company and then goes on to cite reasons as to why it was needed for Europeans to settle in India; all the reasons would benefit the natives. He writes:

> European settlers in India will introduce the knowledge they possess; ...[there would be] free and extensive communication with the various classes of the native inhabitants; ...the European inhabitants the European settlers would gradually deliver the minds from the superstitions and prejudice; ... the settlers being more   on par with the rulers of the country, and aware of the rights belonging to the subjects of a liberal Government, ... would obtain ... many necessary improvements in the [local] laws and judicial system; -- the ... support of the European settlers would ... afford to the natives protection against the impositions and oppression of their landlords and other superiors; ... the   European settlers, from motives of benevolence, public spirit and fellow-feeling towards their native neighbors, would establish schools and other seminaries of education for the

cultivation of the English language throughout the country, and for the diffusion of a knowledge of European arts and sciences."[139]

For Rammohun, European knowledge would greatly benefit the Indians. He writes that an invasion could be avoided if "supported by a large body of European inhabitants; --- [and] a connection [would be formed] between Great Britain and India." If a separation did take place, then there still would exist a large group of "respectable settlers (consisting of Europeans and their descendants, professing Christianity, and speaking the English language in common with the bulk of the people, as well as possessed of superior knowledge, scientific, mechanical, and political)" which "would bring that vast Empire in the east to a level with other large Christian countries in Europe."[140] The settlers and their descendants would enlighten and civilize the

---

[139] Ibid., p. 79.

[140] Ibid., pp. 81-83.

surrounding nations of Asia.[141] Rammohun was supremely confident that certain aspects of western civilization would become intrinsic to India, in the same manner as had Islamic civilization prior to this.

Derozio was one such descendant of European settlers; he was more European than Indian, and yet he identified himself as being a non-native Indian rather than an European. He was conscious of the formation of the new group of East Indians, a body whose numbers were daily increasing. He wrote:

> They are a body, and yet they are not a body. This involves a paradox. But it is cleared up when we remark that they are a body, inasmuch as their numbers are great and are becoming greater daily; and they are not a body, inasmuch as they do not seem to belong to each other. Most of them, at least the better portion, are anxious for their weal, but each individual is as anxious to effect this in his own way.

---

[141] Ibid., pp. 81-83

One will not concede to the other. Every man is jealous of his neighbour, although every man will be glad to ameliorate the condition of his countrymen. ... Let them unite, let them bring themselves together, form associations and societies, learn the sentiments of each other, find out their own value, and ascertain what they are capable of effecting, then, and not till then, will they be enabled to improve their condition. There was the East Indian Dinner Club, but it fell. And what was the cause of this? Nothing less than the baneful want of unison in feeling." ...[142]

Derozio was concerned that many East Indians sent their children to England for reasons of education; and no "parent (how patriotic soever he might be) would educate his children in India merely to try the experiment of improving the tone of the education here thereby." He goes on to write: "The man who has the welfare of his countrymen at heart will endeavor to

---

[142] Derozio, "No. III: Education in India -- Lines to my Brother in Scotland," in *Derozio*, ed. Rosinka Chaudhury, pp. 88-89.

raise funds for their improvement, establish institutions for the same purpose"; he was born in India, and "proud to acknowledge" his country" but "even love of country" would not "hinder" him expressing what he believed to be right.¹⁴³ A whole new community was formed that gained access to all aspects of a pluralistic Indian civilization.

---

¹⁴³ Ibid., p. 89.

Calcutta, the 12th Jan. 1788.
By Order
C. H. BARLO[W]

[Persian/Urdu text]

[Bengali text table]

For SALE at the CIRCULATING LIBRARY.

Some very elegant Bound

QUARTO and OCTAVO BIBLES and PRAYER B[OOKS]
of different sizes.

Also, some complete Sets of

EUROPE BOUND MERCHANTS BOOK[S]
And a variety of STATIONARY, in good order.

www.ingramcontent.com/pod-product-compliance
Lightning Source LLC
Chambersburg PA
CBHW071301040426
42444CB00009B/1822